YOU CHOOSE

CAN YOU SURVIVE A RAGING HURRICANE?

An Interactive Survival Adventure

by Matt Doeden

Published by Capstone Press, an imprint of Capstone
1710 Roe Crest Drive, North Mankato, Minnesota 56003
capstonepub.com

Library of Congress Cataloging-in-Publication Data is available on the Library of Congress website.
ISBN: 9798875240720 (hardcover)
ISBN: 9798875240690 (paperback)
ISBN: 9798875240706 (ebook PDF)

Summary: You Choose lets YOU control the story! Readers choose their own paths while encountering a hurricane in three different scenarios. The outcomes are different as decisions are made throughout the book.

Editorial Credits
Editor: Mandy Robbins; Designer: Heidi Thompson; Media Researcher: Rebekah Hubstenberger; Production Specialist: Tori Abraham

Image Credits
Associated Press: Bob Bridges, 104; Getty Images: Kyle Niemi/US Coast Guard/Handout, 105, Sean Rayford, 106, Visual Capitalist, 101; Shutterstock: Andrey_Popov, 64, Gubin Yury, 16, Hananeko_Studio, 93, Jorge Puente Palacios, 33, Ksenia Shu, cover, Lost_in_the_Midwest, 48, Love Solutions, 54, Romberi, 74, SeventyFour, 37, Shironagasukujira, 66, Sompetch Khanakornpratip, 50, Tan_supa, 82, Triff, 8, 87, vivanvu, 21, Volha Ushanava, 24, Wiparat P (texture background), back cover and throughout

TABLE OF CONTENTS

INTRODUCTION

ABOUT YOUR ADVENTURE

YOU are caught in the middle of a powerful hurricane. Strong winds drive stinging rain and blow debris everywhere. Lightning flashes in the sky as the spinning storm spawns deadly tornadoes. The storm pushes a wall of sea water—a storm surge—onto land, flooding the coast. Can you find shelter? Can you survive nature's fury? Will you live or die?

Chapter One sets the scene. Then you choose which path to read. Follow the directions at the bottom of the page. Your decisions will change your outcome. After you finish one path, go back and read the others for new perspectives and more adventures.

Turn the page to begin your adventure.

CHAPTER 1

STORM RISING

Far out in the Atlantic Ocean, a breeze blows over warm ocean water. Over several days, water evaporates and rises. Clouds form. They grow bigger and bigger. The clouds begin to spin around an area of low air pressure. A tropical storm is forming.

Warm water feeds the storm. It grows and grows. The winds howl around the calm center of the storm, called the eye. It becomes a hurricane, and it's headed your way.

Turn the page.

As you walk down the street, the hurricane is all anyone can talk about. You stop at the library to pick up a book. Two librarians stand behind the counter chatting about the storm.

"Looks like it's going to be a big one," says one librarian. "I heard that there could be a record storm surge! Imagine how strong those winds must be to literally push the ocean water up onto the land. It's crazy!"

The other librarian just shakes her head. "It seems like the storms get worse every year."

You give them a nervous smile as you check out your book and leave them to their discussion. The hurricane is coming no matter what you say or do, but that doesn't change the fact that you have things to do. You want to get through all of your errands long before the storm forces businesses to close up.

Turn the page.

You stop at the grocery store to pick up some supplies. But the shelves are mostly empty. As soon as it was clear that a major hurricane was on the way, people rushed to stores to stock up on necessities. Now you can't even find basic items like toilet paper, batteries, or canned food.

As you arrive home, you see one of your neighbors hammering plywood boards over her windows.

"Need any help?" you ask her.

She wipes the sweat off of her forehead and shakes her head.

"Thanks for the offer, but I've got this. Just a few more things to do here to get the house ready, and then we're heading north."

You wish her luck. Many people are trying to decide whether to stay or go. Some just want to get out of the way of danger. Others insist that they've lived through dozens of hurricanes and that they want to stay to make sure their homes are okay.

WHAT IS A HURRICANE?

Hurricanes are powerful storms that form over the ocean in areas of low air pressure. Warm, humid ocean air fuels these monster storms. They rapidly spin around their center, called the eye. To be a hurricane, a storm must have wind speeds of at least 74 miles (119 kilometers) per hour. But some have speeds higher than 200 miles (322 km) per hour. In North America, areas along the coast of the Gulf of Mexico are at the greatest danger of hurricanes. But states along the Atlantic Ocean are also at risk.

Hurricanes create storm surges by pushing ocean water toward the land. Storm surges and heavy rainfall can cause flooding. Wind can damage trees and buildings. Tornadoes often form in hurricanes, causing more damage.

Turn the page.

You head inside and flip on the Weather Channel to get the latest updates. A young man is pointing to the radar image of the storm, which is still out at sea.

"The hurricane has actually slowed down a bit," he explains. "That might sound like good news, but it's not. It's just gaining more energy out at sea. This is going to be a big one, folks."

The storm is coming. How will you choose to experience it?

To cover the hurricane along the coast for a local TV station, turn to page 15.

To experience the inland strength of the hurricane from your home, turn to page 45.

To fly out to sea to study the storm as a hurricane hunter, turn to page 73.

CHAPTER 2

COVERING THE STORM

After a quick bite to eat, you head out the door and drive to the TV station where you work. When you get there, your camera operator, Tony, is already getting ready.

"All of the highways are jammed," he says, as he packs his camera gear. He brushes his graying hair out of his eyes and hoists his backpack over his shoulder. "It's bumper-to-bumper on every highway out of here. Seems like we're about the only ones foolish enough to stay behind."

Turn the page.

You chuckle. "Oh, I don't think that's true. Some of my neighbors are planning to stay. They seem to think that living here for a few decades makes them immune to hurricanes."

You try to act casual about going out to cover the storm. But the truth is that you're really nervous. You grew up in the Midwest and have never actually been in a hurricane. You've only been out of college and on this job for a few months, and this will be your first really big story since taking this job in south Florida. You wish you were calm, but you've got big-time butterflies in your stomach.

Your producer, Maya, walks into the room. "Are you two ready?" she asks.

Tony grunts something that sounds like, "Yeah."

"I think so," you tell her. "I just hope I'm up to it."

Turn the page.

Maya just stares at you. You've always felt like she doesn't like you. Tony says she has no patience for new reporters. She likes people she knows and trusts. Maybe this will be your way to earn that trust.

"Well, do your best. Get us some good footage. We want to see the effects of the storm firsthand. Maybe get some interviews with people braving the storm. Just use your best judgment. Oh, and the storm is interfering with our internet, so we won't be able to go live. You'll have to bring the footage back manually."

With that, Maya turns and walks out of the room.

"Sheesh, not so much as a 'good luck,'" Tony jokes as he gives you a grin.

Tony is quite a bit older than you and always seems grumpy. But he's never complained about getting paired up with a newbie. He has been a huge help in showing you how to be a pro.

It's still more than an hour until landfall—the point at which the strongest part of the hurricane moves onto land. But the winds outside are already howling.

Sheets of rain slam into the building. The idea that it only gets stronger from here fills you with a mix of excitement and dread.

You slip into a long rain jacket, and the two of you head out of the door. Even the twenty-foot walk to where the news van is parked is an adventure. A gust of wind almost knocks you off your feet, and the rain stings your face. What have you gotten yourself into?

Tony slides into the driver's seat, while you plop down on the passenger's side. He starts the engine and turns to you.

"All right, this is your show. Where are we headed?" he asks.

Turn the page.

You've given that question a lot of thought. You could always go to the shore to cover the incoming storm surge. It would make for great footage, but it's also about the most dangerous place to be. Or you could head downtown to film boarded-up businesses and try to talk to any people brave—or foolish—enough to be out in the middle of all of this. The footage might not be as exciting, but you'd feel a lot safer.

To cover the storm surge, go to page 21.

To go downtown, turn to page 27.

"Let's head to the water," you say. "If Maya wants dramatic footage, that's where we're going to find it."

Tony grunts an agreement and heads toward a popular beach. When you get there, it's all but abandoned. Only a few vehicles are parked in the main parking lot. It's afternoon, but the dark clouds above make it feel much later in the day. Palm trees shake and sway in the strong winds.

Rain and wind batter you as you step out of the van. Tony carries his camera on his shoulder.

Turn the page.

"We could film from that boardwalk," he suggests. "It's close enough to get good shots of the rising water without getting too close."

It's not a bad idea. But you really want to impress Maya. How amazing would it be if you shot the report from the water's edge? Imagine how much more dramatic it would seem if the water was actually lapping at your feet. You can't decide if the idea is genius or reckless. Maybe it's both.

To go to the boardwalk, go to page 23.

To film from the water's edge, turn to page 25.

After a moment's thought, you realize that going down to the water's edge is a terrible idea. The wind, waves, and surge make the situation hard to predict.

"Over there," you say, pointing to the boardwalk.

Tony films as you report on the conditions near the water.

"You can really see how far the water has risen already," you say as you point toward the coastline. "Within a few hours, the ground beneath me will likely be covered with several feet of water."

Tony pans the camera to some nearby buildings. Rows of sandbags line the foundations of the structures. You explain that the heavy bags are meant to help keep water out of the buildings and—hopefully—limit the damage of flooding.

Turn the page.

With your report filed, it's time to move on. Tony calls into the office. They tell him that a lightning strike has started a fire in an old church not far from where you are. You could cover that story, or you could head downtown to find people to interview. Where will you report next?

To head downtown to interview people on the street, turn to page 27.

To go to the church fire, turn to page 29.

"Come on, let's really get up close," you say, half dragging Tony down toward the shore. He's unenthusiastic.

The waves are crashing in—the storm surge has already begun.

You can tell Tony doesn't like the idea, but he goes along with it. The wind whips your rain jackets as Tony points the camera at you. You count down from three and begin your report.

"With landfall just an hour away, the swell of water known as a storm surge has already begun."

You back up slowly so that the water reaches your feet. Tony slowly follows, tracking you with the camera.

"According to the experts, this storm surge could—"

That's when a large wave crashes against your legs, throwing you off-balance.

Turn the page.

You quickly catch yourself—but Tony doesn't. He goes down, and the camera flies off of his shoulder into the water with a splash.

Your first instinct is to dive in after the expensive camera. You could probably find it before the strong current carries it away. But another big wave is coming. Is it worth the risk?

To go after the camera, turn to page 31.

To leave it and get out of the water, turn to page 33.

Landfall is less than half an hour away by the time you get downtown. The normally bustling streets are deserted. Tony parks the van alongside a building, out of the worst of the wind. As the two of you step out into the terrible conditions, you wonder if this was a good idea.

You can barely stand up as gusts of wind blast through the streets. The rain slashes in almost sideways beneath the streetlights. It stings your face and makes it hard to see anything. Suddenly, all the streetlights blink out.

"There goes the power!" Tony shouts over the wind.

You look up and down the street. Nobody is here. The idea of finding someone to interview looks hopeless. Tony films the scene for a few minutes, just in case the footage is useful.

"You know, I think there's a shelter a block or two down the street," Tony says.

Turn the page.

He points toward a tall group of buildings. "Maybe we should just get out of this weather before it gets worse."

As you think about it, you see a pair of headlights coming down the street. Somebody else is out here. Maybe you could flag them down to get an interview.

To head to the shelter, turn to page 35.

To try to flag down the car, turn to page 39.

The church is only about a mile away. It's been at the heart of the neighborhood for more than 100 years, but now flames are crawling up one side of it. Even in the driving rain, the fire has no trouble burning the old timbers that form the building's structure.

You expected to find multiple fire crews out battling the blaze. But there's only one truck here, parked behind a brick wall that blocks the worst of the wind. You speak to one of the firefighters as you watch together.

"There's just nothing we can do," he says. "The department is spread too thin. We're out rescuing people, dealing with gas leaks and other problems. And even if we had more trucks, the wind makes this fire uncontrollable. Some people think that the rain from a hurricane will put out a fire. But if it's burning hot enough, with dry fuel on the inside of the structure, the rain isn't enough."

Turn the page.

Tony is filming the entire time. You're sad that the historic building is burning, but it's going to be a great story.

The weather is getting worse by the minute, though. Landfall is just twenty minutes away. Debris flies through the streets. Lightning flashes in the sky. The ground is flooding—you're already standing in almost an inch of water. Is it time to head back to the safety of the station?

To go back to the station, turn to page 41.

To continue filming, turn to page 42.

Your instinct is to try to save that camera. Without giving it much thought, you lunge toward the spot where it went under. You're not in very deep. It shouldn't be a problem.

Your arm goes into the water up to your elbow . . . your shoulder. Just before the next wave crashes in, you feel the sharp edge of the camera. As your hand closes around it, the wave slams into you with surprising force. It almost knocks you over.

As you struggle to regain your balance, the current pulls you in the opposite direction—back toward the ocean. This time, you can't keep your feet underneath you. Tony lunges to grab you, but it all happens too fast. You topple over with a huge splash.

The current pulls you—hard. Too late, you realize that you're in a fight for your life. Tony is shouting your name, but you're out of reach as the water pulls you.

Turn the page.

The storm surge pushes water in, but there are equally strong undercurrents dragging you back out. You try to swim against the current, but the waves pummel you and make it impossible to keep your head above water. You're being dragged farther from shore by the moment, and your strength is fading fast.

You struggle, but there's no fighting the power of nature. You were reckless in the face of a hurricane's incredible force. And now instead of reporting the headlines, you will be the headline.

THE END

To follow another path, turn to page 12.
To learn more about hurricanes, turn to page 99.

You underestimated the power of the storm surge. Quite suddenly, you realize that you have put both Tony and yourself in danger. You grab Tony by the arm and help him to his feet. Together, you run farther up toward shore—out of the reach of the crashing waves.

"Are you okay?" you ask.

Turn the page.

Tony puts his head in his hands and lets out a deep sigh. "I should never have let you be so reckless. Maya is probably going to fire us after this."

He might be right. Maya was counting on you to be her in-the-field reporter. But now, you've lost a very expensive camera, and you don't have any hurricane footage for her to show on the news. If she didn't like you before, she's going to hate you now."

You're wet and cold and feeling like a failure. Maybe the exciting world of news reporting wasn't for you after all. But you still think you made the right decision by not going after the camera.

THE END

To follow another path, turn to page 12.
To learn more about hurricanes, turn to page 99.

As you stand in the driving rain considering your options, a strong gust of wind blasts you. Above you, you hear a crack as part of a building's roof tears away. It slams down on the pavement only a few dozen feet from where you're standing.

"Dang!" Tony says. "Wish I'd been filming when that happened."

You shake your head in disbelief. What are you doing out here?

"We have to get somewhere safe. Let's go to that shelter."

The two of you make your way through the howling wind and stinging rain, avoiding the debris flying through the air. Finally, you arrive at an old brick armory. You step inside the dimly lit building. The power has gone out, but the armory has an emergency generator.

Turn the page.

People are sheltering downstairs. They are huddled together discussing their worries. Children are crying.

"This is where you can get some interviews," Tony suggests.

You had the same thought. You move around the open space, talking to people about why they are here. One woman was too old to make the drive. Another had car trouble and was stranded. Some couldn't afford to leave.

You spend the night inside then return to the station the next morning. Maya is thrilled with the footage. You watch it together. A young mother stands before you, holding her child.

"We didn't think we needed to leave our home," she says into the camera. "But the hurricane was so much more powerful than I ever imagined. I don't know if we'll have a home to go back to after all of this. But we're lucky to have made it out alive."

Turn the page.

The interview leads the national news that night. It's shown across the country to help people understand the crisis people faced during the disaster. It's a huge step in your young career.

"Good work guys," Maya says—the first time she's ever praised you. "Now get back out there. There's a massive cleanup effort going on right now. Get the footage."

"Welcome to the news business," Tony says, slapping you on your back. "You didn't think you'd get today off, did you?"

THE END

To follow another path, turn to page 12.
To learn more about hurricanes, turn to page 99.

"I see someone," you shout. "Come on!"

You hurry down the street, waving your arms as the headlights approach. As the car pulls up alongside, you realize it's a police cruiser. An officer rolls down her window. "What are y'all doing out here," she says. "Do you need help?"

You lean close to the window. "I'm sorry to bother you, officer. We're just reporters looking for people out braving the hurricane."

The officer just shakes her head. She looks annoyed that you wasted her time.

"Go back to your station," she tells you sternly. "We're busy enough tonight without two more people who need to be rescued."

Your shoulders slump as you watch the cruiser drive off.

"Let's go," Tony says. "At least we got a little footage of the storm. "It's probably not safe to be out here anymore."

Turn the page.

Silently, you head back to the van. This was supposed to be your first big story as a reporter. But you've barely covered it at all. Maya is not going to be happy. Maybe she'll give you one more chance to prove yourself. But you're not counting on it.

THE END

To follow another path, turn to page 12.

To learn more about hurricanes, turn to page 99.

"We got it, Tony," you say. Let's get back to the station before landfall.

Even now, the drive back to the station is an adventure. A blast of wind almost blows you off the road at one point. But you make it. As you head inside, you let out a deep breath.

"I'll be fine never getting hurricane duty again," Tony says as he takes off his soaking wet jacket.

You smile and nod. He's right. Braving a hurricane is dangerous business. But you've got some amazing footage to show on the news tonight. It feels like a big step forward in your career.

"Let's get some rest," Tony says. "Tomorrow, we have to cover cleanup and recovery. It's going to be another busy day."

THE END

To follow another path, turn to page 12.
To learn more about hurricanes, turn to page 99.

Landfall is close, but this is a big story. And there's nobody else out here covering it.

"Let's get a little more footage," you tell Tony.

You prepare to do one more report—this time standing just a few dozen feet in front of the burning building. You brace yourself against the powerful winds, nearly shouting into your microphone just to be heard over the noise of the storm.

But as you speak, a powerful gust rips off a large piece of the church's roof. The flaming debris flies straight at you. You don't have time to run or take cover.

You knew that being out in a hurricane was dangerous. But you never imagined that you'd become a victim quite this way.

THE END

To follow another path, turn to page 12.
To learn more about hurricanes, turn to page 99.

CHAPTER 3

INLAND DISASTER

A crack of thunder rattles the house. Bruno, your black-and-white springer spaniel, whimpers and hides under the kitchen table. He's terrified of loud noises.

"It's all right, Bruno," you tell him, trying to sound calm.

Turn the page.

The dog relaxes a bit, but he's still nervous. You can't blame him. You've known for days that a big hurricane was bearing down on the coast. But you're hundreds of miles from landfall—and far from the ocean. You never imagined that the storm would cause problems here.

You peer out the window as rain pours down. It's coming off the roof so fast that the gutters can't keep up. Sheets of it are spilling over. Through that, you can see the small creek that runs behind your house.

The creek is rarely more than a trickle. Now rushing water is overflowing its banks. The creek is swelling to a height that's getting frighteningly close to the house. Every few minutes, you hear the hum and clunk of your house's sump pump. The underground pump prevents water from seeping up into the house. It rarely runs, but the past day, it's been going almost nonstop.

“It’s a heck of a way to celebrate my eighteenth birthday, eh Bruno?” you mumble.

You were supposed to be out with friends today. But what remains of the hurricane has already dumped eight inches of water on your town—with more to come. Everything is closed. Your mom, a nurse, is one of the few people who actually has to work. And your dad is on the road for business. So it’s just you and Bruno watching the rain. Not the birthday party you had in mind.

Suddenly, the lights blink out. The background noise of the news on the television disappears. Bad just got worse—now the power is out.

At first, that just seems like an inconvenience. But after a few minutes without power, you realize something. The sump pump is no longer humming. Without power, it can’t do its job. You glance outside—the creek has risen even more in just those several minutes.

Turn the page.

“I think we’re in trouble, Bruno,” you say.

What do we do if the house floods? Your heart is racing. Should you leave, or try to protect your belongings? If you do leave, where would you go? Is it even safe to be out in this weather?

To stay and try to save the belongings in the house, go to page 49.

To get out before it floods, turn to page 50.

A quick glance around fills you with dread. If the house floods, you're going to lose everything. So you get to work. You start grabbing stuff—from your video games and electronics to your mom's photo albums—and stack it all on shelves, tables, or anywhere you can get it off the floor.

Then you step into the living room. When your foot hits the carpet, you hear a squish. Water is starting to come in. You rush across the room and look out the back window. There's water surrounding the house. In the back of the house, where the land begins to slope down toward the creek, it's already a few inches high. A large piece of the creek bank is torn away by the torrent of water.

As you watch the land around the house eroding before your eyes, you realize how serious this is. It might not just be your belongings that are in danger. If the ground keeps eroding, the whole house could be at risk.

To flee to a friend's house, turn to page 52.

To keep trying to save your stuff, turn to page 63.

The water is rising so quickly, it's only a matter of time before the house starts to flood. You've seen on the news what rushing floodwaters can do to a house. If the ground around the house starts to erode, the whole thing could collapse. You don't want to be inside if that happens.

"Bruno, come," you call sharply. "We've got to get out of here."

You stuff a few things into a backpack—a water bottle, a flashlight, your favorite video game console, and a few other valuables and slip on a rain jacket.

You hesitate as you stand by the front door. Where are you even going to go? Your friend Trey lives a few blocks away, farther uphill and away from the creek. You could walk there. Otherwise, your dad's sports car is in the driveway. You could take it to the hospital where your mom works. You're not allowed to drive it—it's your dad's pride and joy. But you think he'd understand that this is an emergency.

To walk to Trey's house, turn to page 52.

To take the car, turn to page 54.

"Come on, Bruno," you call. "I don't think it's safe here."

You click Bruno's leash onto his collar. Usually, he's excited to go for a walk. But Bruno hesitates to go outside right now. You slip on a rain jacket and a baseball cap and pull him out the door.

Your feet splash through half an inch of water as you walk down your driveway. Your friend Trey's house is only a few blocks away, but in this weather, that's an adventure. A neighbor's tree has uprooted and fallen over the road. You have to slosh through her yard to get around it. Your shoes are soaked through and covered in mud. Bruno is good and keeps up, but the dog is terrified.

Finally, you get to Trey's house and ring the bell. Nobody answers. You peek into the window and don't see a sign of anyone home.

"Shoot, Bruno," you mutter. "I bet they left to get away from the storm."

Your friend Anna lives nearby too. But going there would mean crossing a low bridge over a creek that could be flooding. Is that a smart idea? You know that Trey's family never locks the back door to their garage. You could let yourself in. But is it okay just to go into a friend's house when they're not there?

To go to Anna's house, turn to page 57.

To let yourself in through the garage, turn to page 66.

"Dad will understand," you tell Bruno as you grab the keys to the shiny red Mustang. "At least I hope he will."

Bruno follows you out into the pouring rain and blustering wind. You dash for the car and get in. Soaking wet, Bruno jumps in after you, getting water all over the passenger seat. Dad's not going to like that. You fire up the engine and carefully back out of the driveway. A few inches of water are pooled up at the end of the driveway, and the car sloshes through the big puddle.

The hospital is only a few miles away. You drive slowly in the pouring rain, struggling to even see where you're going. The wind makes it difficult to keep the car from swerving.

You turn on the radio to get weather updates. A woman is talking about the storm, warning about a tornado sighting just a few miles south of you. You had forgotten that hurricanes can cause tornadoes too—especially inland.

As you drive, you come to a place where the road dips into a small valley. Flooding creek water has covered a small section of the road where it dips into a valley. It's only twenty to thirty feet of road that's covered, and you think it's probably not that deep.

Over the sound of the whooshing windshield wipers and pouring rain, you hear a siren—a tornado warning. Bruno hears it too. The dog cowers in the front seat.

Turn the page.

You could turn around and head south to get to a better road. But that would be heading in the direction of the tornado. Or you could just drive through the water-covered section of road. It's only a small distance. You think you could make it, but you can't know for sure.

To turn around, turn to page 59.

To drive through the water, turn to page 61.

“Let’s go, boy,” you tell Bruno.

He just sits there whimpering as you tug on his leash. His instincts tell him not to go back out into the storm. But you are firm, and he eventually gives in.

You slosh a few more blocks to reach the bridge. It’s just an old wooden bridge for foot traffic. The water is rushing just inches below it. Anna’s house is half a block from the other side, up a steep hill. You can see her driveway from here—and there’s a car parked in it. You’re almost to safety.

With a deep breath, you make your way out onto the wet wood. The rushing water is terrifying, and Bruno won’t budge. He refuses to step out onto the bridge. You scoop the wet dog up in your arms and carry him. He’s shaking. The bridge is solid under your feet, but you don’t want to waste any time.

Turn the page.

You get about halfway across when a bolt of lightning flashes in the sky. A second later, a huge crack of thunder rattles the bridge under your feet.

It's too much for Bruno. In a panic, the dog wriggles loose from your grip. You lurch forward, trying to hold onto him. But you watch in horror as he goes over the handrail—into the rushing water. The leash yanks free from your grasp as you watch Bruno splash into the rushing current.

To jump in after Bruno, turn to page 69.

To trust Bruno can save himself, turn to page 70.

You don't like either choice. But you know that driving through moving water is one of the most dangerous things you could do in this situation. You'll take your chances in the other direction.

You turn the car around and head south. The sky is dark. You watch the horizon for signs of a tornado, but you don't see anything.

"We'll be okay, Bruno," you say, mostly to convince yourself.

You grip the steering wheel tightly as you drive through the downpour. Your windshield wipers can't keep up with the rain, and at times, you can barely tell where the road is. But you make it.

You park the car in the hospital's parking ramp. A wave of relief washes over you as you finally get out of the rain. That's when you realize that you can't bring Bruno inside with you.

"Sit tight, boy," you tell him as you scratch his ears. "I'll come back out and wait with you."

Turn the page.

You go inside and head to the floor where your mom works. She wraps you up in a big hug as you tell her about the house.

"Thank goodness you got out," she says. "Your dad won't mind at all. You're much more important than a car."

You don't know what you'll find when you finally get back home. You don't even know when you'll be able to get there. But you're safe now. You'll go back to the parking garage and wait out the storm here, however long that takes.

THE END

To follow another path, turn to page 12.
To learn more about hurricanes, turn to page 99.

The siren blares. You glance back over your shoulder but can't see anything through the heavy rain. The thought of driving toward a tornado terrifies you. A few inches of water seems a lot less dangerous.

You drive slowly toward the spot where the road dips down into the water. Slowly, you roll your way in. The car's tires go in an inch . . . two. You keep going, slow but steady. As you reach the halfway point, you feel the car's back end start to pull to the left.

Panic sets in. The water is deeper than you expected, and the current is dragging the car off of the road. You try to steer the other direction. You step on the gas, trying to power your way out. But it's hopeless. The car twists and spins as the rushing water drags it.

Your mind races. What should you do? Is it safer to get out of the car? You can't decide. The water drags the car along faster and faster.

Turn the page.

Too late, you realize it's pulling you toward a steep bank. The water is up to the windshield now. It's spilling into the car through the doors.

You try to open the door to escape, but the pressure of the water outside the car makes that impossible. You're sinking, and you can't get out.

As the red Mustang slips into the rushing creek, you realize that you took a terrible risk, and now you're going to pay for it with your life.

THE END

To follow another path, turn to page 12.
To learn more about hurricanes, turn to page 99.

You can't give up now. But instead of stacking things on shelves, you start moving it to your dad's sports car, which is parked in the driveway. You're not supposed to drive it, but you think he'll understand in this case.

You make several runs into and out of the house. Bruno follows you outside. He's running up and down the yard, barking at the rain. He is clearly distressed.

"One more load, Bruno," you shout as you run back inside.

Things are getting worse. The creek has risen even higher. Several trees have tipped into its banks.

Suddenly, a tornado siren goes off in the distance. That's when you remember that hurricanes can spur tornadoes, especially inland, where you are.

Turn the page.

The floor is no longer just wet. It's a pool. You wade into knee-deep cold water, desperate to rescue a few last items. That's when you hear a terrible crack. The rushing water rips away another huge chunk of land—land that the house sits on. The house splits in two, with half of it falling into the rushing floodwaters—the half that you're in.

You feel yourself falling and then crash into a wet, churning mix of debris and water. It all happens so fast, you never had a chance. You struggle in vain to keep your head above water as the ceiling forces you under. Your last thought is that you're glad that at least Bruno was outside.

THE END

To follow another path, turn to page 12.

To learn more about hurricanes, turn to page 99.

You lead Bruno around to the back of the garage. Sure enough, the door is unlocked. You step inside and flick the light switch. But nothing happens.

You groan. Of course, the power is out.

You have to feel your way through the pitch-black garage, searching for the door that leads inside. You bang your shin into a lawn mower and walk straight into a low-hanging shelf. But you manage to find the door. You step inside. Dim light filters in through the windows, but the house is otherwise dark.

Bruno is wet and muddy, so you clip his leash to a hook in the entryway. You kick off your shoes and walk inside.

You sit for a moment, just catching your breath. But your mind races. Your house's sump pump was out. That means Trey's is out too. The family doesn't have a basement, just a small crawl space. You walk down the hall and peek inside.

Sure enough, the crawl space is slowly filling with water. Eventually, it will rise and start flooding the ground floor.

There's probably no hope for your house, but you can help Trey. You find a few ice-cream buckets and start bailing the water out of the crawl space.

It takes about fifteen minutes of bailing before the water is mostly gone. After that, you have to fill up another bucket every twenty minutes or so.

Turn the page.

You spend the day doing that. Finally, that evening, the power comes back on. The lights flick on, and the pump starts humming,

You plop down next to a sleeping Bruno.

"Phew, that was work," you say with a sigh.

You're awfully glad you let yourself in. You couldn't save your house from flooding. But you saved this one.

THE END

To follow another path, turn to page 12.
To learn more about hurricanes, turn to page 99.

"Bruno!" you shout.

Without hesitation, you leap over the railing, into the rushing water. You immediately realize your mistake.

The cold water takes your breath away, and the current instantly sucks you under. Fully dressed, you have no chance in the violently churning floodwaters. You surface for a moment, gasping for breath. But it feels impossible to stay afloat in your wet, heavy clothes and shoes.

Bruno is a great swimmer. He'll at least have a chance to survive. But your rash decision will bring your story to an end.

THE END

To follow another path, turn to page 12.
To learn more about hurricanes, turn to page 99.

You resist the instinct to dive in after Bruno. That would be a deadly decision. You know he's a good swimmer. He struggles against the raging current.

"Swim Bruno!" you shout. "Swim!"

You quickly lose sight of him as the water sweeps him away. Your heart aches, knowing you may never see him again. But you hold out hope he'll make his way back to shore. You know he'll have a better shot than you would have in that roiling water.

With tears in your eyes, you cross the bridge. A minute later, you're knocking on Anna's door.

Anna's family welcomes you. You spend the evening and night there as the worst of the storm finally passes.

You meet your mom the next day, back at home. You're devastated to see that part of the house collapsed into the flooded creek.

“We’ll have to rebuild,” your mom says, trying to sound positive. “The important thing is that we’re both alive.”

You nod, silently. Your thoughts are on Bruno. You imagine you hear him barking off in the distance. It sounds so real.

Then you realize . . . it is real. Bruno, covered in mud and with a bloody snout, comes bounding around the corner. He made it! You all did. You’ve never been so relieved in all your life.

THE END

To follow another path, turn to page 12.
To learn more about hurricanes, turn to page 99.

CHAPTER 4

FLYING INTO THE STORM

You've been watching hurricane news coverage for days. Your neighbors are either leaving the area or preparing their houses for landfall. For most of them, the hurricane is just a storm. For you, it's much more. That's because you're a hurricane hunter. You don't run from a hurricane. You see it as an opportunity for research. As the storm has built in strength, you've prepared for a close encounter.

Turn the page.

"Are you ready for this?" asks Dr. Hancock as you step on board the WP-3D Orion. The scientific airplane is loaded with high-tech weather sensors designed to measure every aspect of the hurricane that's bearing down on the coast.

You give her a smile. The truth is you're nervous, but you don't want to show it. "Of course, I am," you reply, hoping to sound confident.

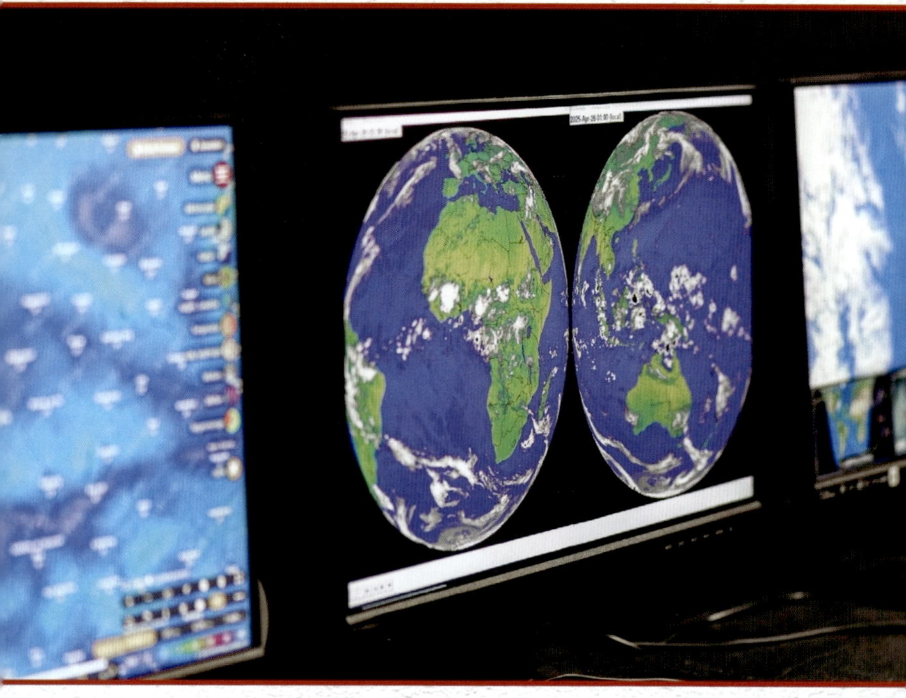

As you step on board the plane, scientists and technicians are busy making the final preparations for your flight. Your mission is to fly directly into the hurricane. It sounds crazy, but there's no better way to study these amazing storms. The data you collect will help weather experts forecast exactly where and when the storm will make landfall. It will also help scientists better understand how these storms form, strengthen, and evolve.

The final preparations are in place. The sensors are up and running. The crew is ready to go. The flight tower gives you clearance to take off. It's the opportunity of a lifetime. It's also dangerous. But you're ready and willing to take the risk.

To pilot the airplane, turn to page 76.

To work as a scientist collecting data, turn to page 78.

You grip the controls as you race down the runway. As the plane gains speed, the wings provide lift, and soon, you're soaring through the sky. Your copilot, Jaylen, flips a switch.

"And we're off," he says into the intercom. "Enjoy the smooth sailing while you can, everyone. It'll get bumpy soon enough."

He's right. The first hour of the flight is easy. But as you approach the giant storm, the ride gets rocky. When you finally descend into the outer clouds of the hurricane, you can feel the storm's power. You look over at Jaylen, who is aggressively biting his fingernails.

"Don't worry," you tell him. "The plane is designed for these kinds of winds. It's really just wind shear that we're worried about—rapid changes in wind direction at different altitudes. Dr. Hancock is monitoring that."

Right on cue, Dr. Hancock calls up. "I'm seeing multiple hook echoes between us and the eye," she says.

Hook echoes are features on radar. They show spots where winds are swirling in a vortex—much like a tornado. The rapidly changing directions of strong winds could be dangerous to the plane.

The team really wants to get into the eye for the best measurements. Can you navigate around the dangerous areas? Or should you avoid them and abandon your hope of reaching the eye?

To continue toward the eye of the storm, turn to page 81.

To focus on the safer edges of the storm, turn to page 84.

You thought you'd be nervous. The idea of flying into a hurricane seems terrifying. But you're so busy getting things ready that you don't have time for nerves.

Dr. Hancock is in charge of the scientific mission. You're a meteorology student who jumped at the chance to join her team. Your main job is to deploy the dropsonde devices. The small cylinders are packed with weather sensors. You'll shoot them out of the plane through a long tube at different places. Once they're out, a small parachute allows them a slow descent, meaning they can collect a lot of data.

You watch as the plane approaches the giant storm. The ride starts to get rocky, but you're ready for it. As the plane enters the outer edges of the storm, the scientific work really begins.

"Let's get started," Dr. Hancock says, nodding toward you.

You load the first dropsonde and let it go. Whoosh! It's out of the plane. You quickly check your monitor.

"It's working!" you shout. Sure enough, the little sensor is sending back data.

As you fly deeper into the storm, you release more. You watch as the air pressure drops the closer you get to the eye. It makes sense. The storm spins around an area of very low pressure. It's what drives the whole thing.

A bolt of lightning streaks across the sky, followed by a crack of thunder. Suddenly, the plane lurches and drops. It feels like your stomach is in your throat.

You look toward the cockpit. The two pilots appear to be scrambling, trying to fight the rough ride. You overhear one of them saying that two engines have blown out.

Turn the page.

You don't know a lot about planes, but you know that can't be good.

The other scientists are scrambling to their seats and buckling in. You only need about ten more seconds to release another dropsonde. Should you finish the task or buckle in right away?

To buckle in, turn to page 86.

To try to release one more sensor, turn to page 96.

You make a small course change to avoid the areas of the storm that look the worst. As you fly through the clouds, flashes of lightning pop all around you.

Behind you, the team is working hard to collect data. Dr. Hancock is monitoring the radar and other stations. Her interns, Susan and Juan, are deploying small sensors called dropsondes. They use a tube to drop them out of the plane. The sensors use radio transmitters to send back their position along with a wide range of weather data as they drop to the ocean.

"We're getting great data!" Juan calls up.

Just then, a gust of wind slams the plane.

"We've got strong wind shear," Jaylen says. "I think we got too close to that hook echo!"

You fight the controls as the plane takes a sudden dip. A bolt of lightning cracks right on top of you.

Turn the page.

The bolt passes through the wing of the plane. Suddenly, the plane lurches.

“We just lost engine three,” Jaylen calls out. “Engine two is out as well!”

With half of your engines out, you’re helpless to control the plane. You hear screaming from the back as the plane begins a sharp drop.

"Three thousand feet," Jaylen reports. "Twenty-six hundred . . . dropping fast."

Frantically, you try to get the engines to refire. But if you can't, the plane is too heavy to fly with just two engines. You've got hundreds of pounds of sensors and weather gear. If you dump it all, you might be light enough. But you'll lose every bit of data you've collected. You're running out of time.

To keep trying to fire the engines, turn to page 88.

To dump your gear, turn to page 89.

"I don't like the look of that radar," you tell Jaylen. "If we get into strong wind shear, we might not be able to keep the plane steady."

"I think we can handle it," Jaylen replies. "This plane is built for those kinds of conditions. I think you can push it a little."

You shake your head. "No, we'll just collect what we can from the edges of the storm. There's no sense taking risks."

"Yeah, why would hurricane hunters be willing to take risks?" Jaylen mutters, sarcastically.

You don't let it bother you. "My job is to keep my passengers safe," you reply.

You spend the next hour on a path that traces the outer edges of the hurricane. Dr. Hancock begs you to go deeper.

"We really need to get closer to the eye," she insists.

"We're not doing that much good out here," she continues. "If you're not willing to fly us in, maybe you could hand over the controls to your copilot. He seems willing and capable."

You can feel the pressure from the entire crew. All of them are upset with you. Could you be wrong? Are you playing it too safe?

To change your mind, turn to page 92.

To refuse to go any deeper, turn to page 95.

It's not worth risking your life. So you quickly sit down and buckle in.

You're glad you did. The plane bucks and rattles as the pilots struggle to refire an engine that had gone out.

You come close to throwing up as the strong hurricane winds toss the plane. But after a few minutes, the pilots solve the problem. Soon, they climb up to a less turbulent altitude.

"Back to work, everyone," says Dr. Hancock. You release several more sensors. Finally, the plane breaks through into the eye. It's suddenly calm and mostly clear.

"Amazing," your fellow intern, Juan, gasps, gazing out a window.

You take a quick peek then release your final dropsonde. The data from the little sensors is already pouring in.

You spend a few minutes in the eye, helping others take readings. You even manage to snap some amazing photos on your phone. It's one of the most inspiring experiences of your life. But it's time to get back. You'll spend weeks going over all of the data you've collected.

Turn to page 91.

"Come on . . . come ON!" you shout as you keep trying the engines.

The plane continues to drop. You're under two thousand feet now. You can see the ocean surface below. You're running out of time.

Just when you think there's no hope, it happens. Engine two fires back up. That's three engines—enough to keep the plane in the sky. You level off before rising back up toward the clouds.

For a moment, everyone is silent. Then the whole team breaks out in a cheer. You don't want to risk this happening again. Clearly, this storm is too dangerous to fly into.

"Hold on tight everyone," you say over the intercom. "I'm going to take us back home."

Turn to page 91.

“We’re too heavy!” you announce. “We need to dump our gear!”

You expect the scientists on board to protest. But they sense the danger.

Everyone quickly gets to work. They open a hatch and start tossing out the heaviest gear. Computers, expensive radar equipment, even high-definition cameras. It all falls to the ocean below.

While they do that, you flip a switch to dump some of the airplane’s fuel. You’ll be cutting your mission short and won’t need it. With two dead engines, every bit matters.

The plane drops to fifteen thousand feet before it finally starts to level off. The team tosses out a few more precious sensors, and the load is finally light enough for you to begin ascending.

“Okay, we’ve got it,” you tell them.

Turn the page.

Their reply is silence. Everyone is heartbroken that the mission will be a failure.

You're disappointed too. But your first responsibility is to bring everyone back safely. You didn't achieve what you wanted, but at least everyone will make it home.

THE END

To follow another path, turn to page 12.
To learn more about hurricanes, turn to page 99.

The plane gains altitude then heads back out of the storm. A few hours later, your wheels touch down safely. The team quickly gets to work sending their data to the National Weather Service.

"This will make a difference in forecasting how strong this storm will be," Dr. Hancock says. "Good job out there, everyone. We did it!"

As you set foot on solid ground, you look at the sky. It's filled with clouds right now, but it's calm. In a day or two, it's going to look very different.

"What do you think?" Juan asks as he exits the plane. "Would you do it again?"

"I would," you say, surprising yourself. As terrifying as it was, you wouldn't miss another chance to fly into the heart of a hurricane.

THE END

To follow another path, turn to page 12.
To learn more about hurricanes, turn to page 99.

Maybe they're right. This is a hurricane hunting mission. Yes, you want to stay safe, but you have to take risks to get the data you need.

"Okay," you finally agree. "I'll take us in. But understand that if it gets too bad in there, I'm coming right back out. And keep an eye on that radar. Don't let me get anywhere near that hook echo. Clear?"

Dr. Hancock smiles. "Got it!" she replies.

Your hands shake a bit as you steer the plane deeper into the storm. Soon, you are swallowed up in dark clouds. Flashes of lightning pop all around you. Strong winds blast the plane, but it's built to withstand them.

Flying into the heart of the storm is both terrifying and thrilling at the same time. You haven't been this nervous flying a plane since your first solo flight years ago.

The team busily collects valuable data on the storm. They drop small sensors called dropsondes out of the plane that take a range of measurements. Detailed radar images give a unique view of the hurricane and how updrafts—winds that carry air from the ocean surface up into the clouds—help feed the storm and make it bigger.

Turn the page.

The crew was hoping to make it to the eye of the storm, but you just don't have the nerve to try that. They'll have to be satisfied with this much. And now you know that maybe flying into hurricanes isn't for you. In the future, you'll leave that to pilots who are a bit more willing to accept risk.

THE END

To follow another path, turn to page 12.
To learn more about hurricanes, turn to page 99.

You clench your jaw and shake your head. "Please take what readings you can from here. Soon, we'll be headed back to land."

Dr. Hancock just stares at you for a few moments. Finally, she sighs and walks back.

You spend another twenty minutes flying through the edge of the hurricane. As you come in and out of clouds, you can see the ocean surface below. Even from way up here, it looks violent.

As your fuel reserves reach about half, you guide the plane back in the direction of land. You know you have unhappy scientists behind you. And the data they've collected might not be worth much. But were you wrong to avoid risk?

One thing's for sure. You know you'll never be asked to join another hurricane hunting mission.

THE END

To follow another path, turn to page 12.
To learn more about hurricanes, turn to page 99.

You've almost got the dropsonde ready to go, you'll buckle up in just a moment. You finish loading the small sensor and send it out of the plane. Success!

You turn to head back to your seat. But just as you do, a powerful gust of wind slams into the plane. The gust sends the plane into a sudden dive.

The rest of the scientists and crew are buckled in. But you're not. The sudden movement lifts you off of your feet. You're thrown headfirst into a table. Everything goes black as you slam into it.

You're knocked out cold for several minutes. When you finally regain consciousness, the plane is on its way out of the hurricane.

"We had to cut the mission short," says Dr. Hancock as she kneels over you, putting a bandage on your head. "We need to get you to a hospital right away."

You're groggy and in lots of pain. But the worst part of it is that the mission is a failure because of your bad decision. You're pretty sure you'll never be invited on another one of these flights. It was your one and only chance, and you blew it.

THE END

To follow another path, turn to page 12.
To learn more about hurricanes, turn to page 99.

CHAPTER 5

UNDERSTANDING HURRICANES

Hurricanes and typhoons are a type of storm called a tropical cyclone. The only difference between them is where they form. Hurricanes start in the Atlantic Ocean or central Pacific Ocean. Typhoons start in the northwest Pacific Ocean, closer to Asia. The term tropical cyclones is used for these storms in the South Pacific and Indian Ocean. All three are the same thing.

Hurricanes start as tropical depressions. These are areas of low air pressure over warm ocean water.

If conditions are right, winds called updrafts carry warm, wet air up into high altitudes, where it forms clouds. When that happens, the storm can grow into a tropical cyclone. If wind speeds reach at least 74 miles (119 km) per hour, it's a hurricane (or a typhoon).

The storm spins around the low-pressure center of the cyclone, called the eye. The faster the winds, the stronger the hurricane.

Scientists classify hurricanes into categories. Category 1 hurricanes are the weakest. Category 5 hurricanes are the strongest, with winds of at least 157 miles (253 km) per hour.

Hurricane Allen in 1980 was the strongest hurricane ever recorded. It had sustained winds of 190 miles (306 km) per hour.

Hurricane Category	Wind Speed	Damage Summary
1	75–95 mph *119–153 km/h*	Some Damage: Minor damage to homes & short-term power loss
2	96–110 mph *154–177 km/h*	Extensive damage: Major roof damage to buildings & near-total power loss
3	111–129 mph *178–208 km/h*	Devastating damage: Electricity & water unavailable for up to several weeks
4	130–156 mph *209–251 km/h*	Catastrophic damage: Severe damage to homes, with long-lasting power outages & road blockages
5	157 mph+ *252 km/h+*	Catastrophic damage: High % of homes destroyed; area uninhabitable for weeks or months

The deadliest U.S. hurricane happened in 1900. The Great Galveston Hurricane struck Texas with little warning, killing around 8,000 people.

The Bhola Cyclone struck the Asian nation of East Pakistan (present-day Bangladesh) in 1970. Terrible flooding led to as many as half a million deaths.

In 2005, Hurricane Katrina ravaged the city of New Orleans, Louisiana. And in 2024, hurricanes Helene and Milton struck the southeastern United States within two weeks of each other, causing massive damage.

TRUE HURRICANE SURVIVAL STORIES

Jeff Masters, Hurricane Hugo (1989)

Meteorologist Jeff Masters was part of a hurricane hunting team that flew into Hurricane Hugo in 1989. The flight started normally. But then, a key radar system stopped working. Without it, the crew had no way of spotting the most dangerous parts of the storm.

The plane flew into dangerously shifting winds. It was tossed, sending it into dives and terrible turbulence. One of its four engines burned out and another was covered in debris.

The plane barely made it into the storm's eye. There, the crew dumped gear to lighten the plane so that they could fly out of the hurricane. They made it, but it was an extremely close call.

Leatha Groomes, Hurricane Katrina (2005)

Hurricane Katrina caught many people off guard. The city of New Orleans, Louisiana, was hit especially hard.

Leatha Groomes and her family fled to the roof of their house to escape the floodwaters from the storm surge. They waited there for three days. Their food and water was almost gone. They had no medicine for Leatha's mother, who suffered from diabetes. Finally, a rescue helicopter spotted them. They all made it out safely.

Dorothy Brooks, Hurricane Helene (2024)

Seventy-six-year-old Dorothy Brooks had nowhere to go when Hurricane Helene hit in 2024. As the storm surge rushed in, her house was flooding. The water was so high that she couldn't even open a door to get out. She had to crawl out of a window. There, she saw a neighbor being swept away by the rushing water. Another neighbor had climbed on top of a pick-up truck to escape the water. Brooks held on to that window frame until the U.S. Coast Guard finally came to rescue her.

HURRICANE SURVIVAL KIT

Hurricanes can strike with shocking force. In the past, people didn't always have much warning. But now, weather services know days ahead of time when a disaster is coming. That gives people plenty of time to gather some basic survival supplies.

Food and Water

A hurricane can disrupt the supply of basics like food and water. Keeping some canned food and bottled water can be a lifesaver in the days following a hurricane. And don't forget a can opener!

Flashlight

Floods and high winds can knock out the power during a hurricane. A flashlight with fresh batteries will help you find your way in the dark.

Radio

A battery-powered radio can give you the news you need to make good decisions following a disaster.

First-aid Kit

A basic first-aid kit will help you deal with minor medical emergencies.

Hand Sanitizer

Flooded areas can be filled with germs and filth. Protect yourself with hand sanitizer.

Cell Phone

Cell service may be spotty after a natural disaster, but if it's working, a phone can be a vital lifeline.

Whistle

A loud emergency whistle can get the attention of rescuers.

STAYING SAFE IN A HURRICANE

How can you stay safe in a hurricane? Follow a few steps to give yourself the best chance.

Before the Storm

- Check for evacuation orders. If you can get out of the storm's path, do it. If not, look for a storm shelter.
- Prepare your home. Clean gutters. Add shutters or plywood over windows to protect them from wind and debris. Stock up with supplies.
- Stay tuned to the latest news, warnings, and alerts.

During the Storm

- Stay in an interior room, away from windows.
- Move to a higher floor or rooftop if the home starts to flood.
- Don't walk or drive into moving water. It can sweep you away.

GLOSSARY

debris (duh-BREE)—scattered pieces left after something has been destroyed

depression (di-PRE-shuhn)—in weather, a term to describe an area of low air pressure; depressions can serve as the starting point for a hurricane

dropsonde (DROP-sond)—a device that scientists drop into hurricanes and tropical storms to measure and study them

eye (EYE)—the calm, clear zone at the center of a hurricane

inland (IN-luhnd)—away from the coastline

radar (RAY-dar)—a sensor that can detect precipitation, such as rain, in the air and determine how it is moving

storm surge (STORM SURJ)—a sudden, strong rush of water that happens as a hurricane moves onto land

READ MORE

Collins, Ailynn. *Hurricanes and the Environment*. North Mankato, MN: Capstone Press, 2025.

Foxe, Steve. *Deadly Natural Disasters*. North Mankato, MN: Capstone Press, 2024.

Murrell, Diana. *Hurricane Hunters*. Mendota Heights, MN: Apex Editions, 2025.

INTERNET SITES

NASA Science: How Do Hurricanes Form?
spaceplace.nasa.gov/hurricanes/en/

National Geographic Kids: Hurricanes
kids.nationalgeographic.com/science/article/hurricane

Ready Kids: Hurricanes
ready.gov/kids/disaster-facts/hurricanes

ABOUT THE AUTHOR

Matt Doeden is a freelance author and editor from Minnesota. He's written numerous children's books on sports, music, current events, the military, extreme survival, and much more. His book *It's Outta Here* was included on Bank Street's Best Books of the Year List in 2022. He lives in Minnesota with his wife and two children.